He's Not Your friend

BY
SHED KING JR

Copyright ©2021 Shed King Jr.

All rights reserved. No part of this publication may be reproduced, distributed, or transmitted in any form or by any means, including photocopying, recording, or other electronic or mechanical methods, without the prior written permission of the publisher, except in the case of brief quotations embodied in critical reviews and certain other noncommercial uses permitted by copyright law.

ISBN-978-1-951300-01-2

Liberation's Publishing – West Point - Mississippi

He's Not Your friend

BY
SHED KING JR

Table of Content

Introduction 7

Chapter 1 Recognize Your Enemies 11

Chapter 2 Transformation to Light 21

Chapter 3 He Teams Up with Self 29

Chapter 4 He Teams Up with The World System 41

Chapter 5 He's Seeking to Kill You 49

Chapter 6 Understand Who You Are Fighting 57

Chapter 7 He's Not to Be Feared 65

He's Not Your Friend

Introduction

In life you will find out that no one is exempt from the temptations of life. We all have things on the inside of us that will cause us to lean towards doing the wrong thing. Perfection cannot and will not be found within the heart and mind of mankind. The Bible declares that all have sinned and fallen short of the glory of God (Romans 3:23). It is something about living in this fleshly body that even when you make up in your heart and mind to do right, wrong it always present. You have every intention to stop doing what you are doing; make a change for the better. As soon as you decide this something opposes you almost immediately.

I remember in my early years of walking with the Lord Jesus Christ, I told myself that I was going to be faithful in going to Bible Class. That very next Bible Class after my vow, that Wednesday, I was heading out to Bible Class and got a flat tire. You might say, "it doesn't take long to fix a flat." You're right. It doesn't. I have always maintained the attitude that I hate to be late for anything.

I hated it to the point that I wouldn't go if I was late. In getting the flat I found myself getting angry and frustrated to the point I said there is no need of going to Bible Class tonight. So, I didn't go and when Sunday came Pastor Williams asked where I was Wednesday night. I told him I got a flat and since I was going to be late, I said there was no need to come. I would rather stay home than getting there late.

Pastor Williams looked at me and said, "I truly understand how you feel about being late, but have you ever heard it said better late than never?" My reply was, "Yes, but that is how I feel." He looked at me and shook his head and said to me "you are allowing your feelings to block your blessings from God." Then it came to me the commitment I just made. I said I was going to be faithful in going to Bible Class and the very first week after making my commitment I missed Bible Class.

Have you ever told yourself you were going to do better? Well, if you have then brace yourself because a test is on the way. Hosea 4:6 tells us that my *people are destroyed because of a lack of knowledge,* and Paul tells us in 2 Corinthian 2:11 *for we are not ignorant of his devices.* Let's take a closer look at why we struggle so often to keep our commitments, and the challenges we face in our day-to-day battles in this fleshly body we live in.

He's Not Your Friend

Chapter 1 Recognize Your Enemies

We go through life thinking that everything and everybody is on our side. When people are smiling in our face saying all the right things, and doing all the things we like, we tend to believe they are on our side. When you have a real hard time saying no to yourself or you try to get your hands on everything you want you feel things are in your favor. When you are caught up in the fortune, fame, power, and riches of life and you will do whatever it takes to get your hands on it.

When you go to church and that feeling you use to get is gone, or someone is sitting in your seat, or someone is singing your song, or someone is preaching a sermon you preached, or someone is using the same phrases you use in a prayer, or you just aren't in the mood to be bothered today. Do any of these things sound familiar to you? If you are a child of God, it does. You have to always keep in mind that there are things about you, in you, and around you that are enemies to God. In this chapter we are going to discuss three enemies that plague us the most.

Enemy number 1: SELF Romans 8:7 reads, "because the carnal mind is enmity against God, for it is not subject to the law of God, neither indeed can be". Take a moment to reflect back to the moment when you accepted the Lord Jesus Christ as your Lord and Savior. Most of us found ourselves in the midst of a difficult situation that we couldn't seem to get out of. We found ourselves at a point where we needed help because we just kept making matters worse for ourselves. We called on our friends, and they couldn't help. We sought other type of counsel, and that didn't help.

We were at our breaking point, ready to give

up and then we turned our lives over to God and he began to work things out for us. We were happy about the changes that were taking place in our lives while praising and giving the glory to God. After the great deliverance from God what happened? Did we make a total change, or did we make a partial change? I wonder if we were truly aware of what happened to us at the time.

God didn't remove your nature out of you he just placed another nature down inside you and left the decision in your hands to which nature is going to be the strongest in you. The carnal mind is an enemy of God and you still possess it, but just because you possess it doesn't mean it has to rule your life. All the things you loved to do before you got saved are still in there. What God did was create a dichotomy on the inside of you by placing his spirit in you and now there is war taking place in you.

When you read Romans chapter 7:14-25 you will see how the Apostle Paul argues about this flesh/carnal mind that we have to deal with every day of our lives. This struggle is real, and it is alive in you. Paul also states in Colossians chapter three that we are to mortify our members which are on the earth.

What he is saying is we need to bring our bodies under control and treat our fleshly desires as though they are dead. When those sinful desires begin to rise up in you God's spirit will give you the strength to fight them off. So, keep it at your attention your flesh/carnal mind is an enemy of God and you are responsible for keeping your own self in line.

Enemy number 2: The worlds system James 4:4 reads "ye adulterers and adulteress, know ye not that the friendship of the world is enmity with God? Whosoever therefor will be a friend of the world is the enemy of God." How easy is it to get caught up in the fortune, fame, power, and prestige that the world has to offer? I believe it's safe to say that everyone wants to be rich, and for those of you who are modest and would say you don't want to be rich, even you would love to have more than what you already have now. There is something about this flesh that we live in to where it is never satisfied. You can ask the richest or wealthiest person on the planet if they have enough and you will find the answer to be, "no." They are on a quest to make more.

A good question to ask yourself is, "When is enough, enough? At what point in our lives do we learn to be content? Paul makes this statement in Philippians 4:11. "for I have learned in whatsoever state I am, there with to be content". He also states in 1 Timothy "godliness with contentment is great gain". For some reason or another the flesh says with all the things the world has to offer why should I settle for less than what I can achieve.

Most of us have set goals in life. We have plans and we work hard to achieve our goals. Where does God fit in our plans? Think back to when you were in elementary school and the teacher asked the class what do you want to be when you grow up? The class responded by saying lawyers, doctors, policemen, and firemen, and other noble professions. It is embedded in us as children to be all we can and get all we can. The system of the world is designed to pull you away from God, and yet as his children we fail to realize it.

Fortune, fame, power, and prestige are designed to cause people to take a look at me, look at what I've done, look at what I got. You take your eyes off of God and start looking at self. The more you look at self the more you fall in love with self. The further you begin to drift away from God.

There are more things about the system of the world. I am going to explain them when I cover our next enemy. The remainder of the book will cover our third enemy. It will deal with how he uses enemy number one and two against us.

Enemy number 3: Satan John 10:10 reads

"the thief cometh not, but to kill, steal, and destroy." In this passage Satan is known as a thief. but there are other names that he is known as well. The devil, the dragon, the evil one, the angel of the abyss, the ruler of this world, the prince of the power of the air, the god of this world, Apollyon, Abaddon, Belial, Beelzebub, and the accuser of the brethren. No matter which way you know him he means you no good whether you are a child of God or not. If you are a child of God, he wants to steal, kill, or destroy you. If you are not a child of God, he wants to keep you from becoming one. Either way Satan will never be a friend to man.

Everything he does is designed with one thing in mind, and that is to stop God's plan, and he will use whomever he can accomplish his goal. 2 Corinthians 2:11 reads "lest Satan should get an advantage of us, for we are not ignorant of his devices." Satan's methods are designed ultimately to silence the gospel. He seeks to stop the spread of God's word.

What makes this so terrifying is that Satan knows that his time is coming to an end. It would be different if he had just accepted his punishment. That would have been the end of it, but he has the mentality that a lot of people have. If I have to suffer, I am not going to suffer alone.

Some people seek to pull others down with them. Just as Satan is seeking to pull others down with him. That is a selfish and self-centered attitude. The individual with that attitude is very dangerous. That's why it is so important for us to be able to recognize when he is on the attack. He is a shrewd taskmaster. He knows how to set a trap, dig a ditch, place obstacles, and put irritating people in your way to slow you down. He knows what he is doing, and he knows how to get it done.

As Gods children how fast can we recognize his traps? The scripture teaches that the word of God is a lamp unto my feet, and a light unto my path. Also, one more thing to think about before I close out this chapter. If Satan can't get you to do the wrong thing, he will get you to do the right thing the wrong way. We will see this and others as we move forward in the next chapters discussing his methods of attack.

He's Not Your Friend

Chapter 2 Transformation to Light

In understanding how Satan attacks we uncover that he not only goes after individuals, but he also will go after groups of people. Satan knows that there are two types of people in the world, leaders, and followers. His primary concern is to go after the leaders in the world. If he gets the leaders to fall then the followers will fall right behind them. It is of the utmost importance for leaders chosen by God to understand that they are under constant attack from Satan.

I believe that the most affective of his methods is his transformation to light. In 2 Corinthians 11: 13-15 the Apostle Paul deals with the idea of false apostles and deceitful workers transforming themselves into apostles of Christ. He goes on to say don't marvel over their workings, because Satan himself does the same thing. It's not a great thing if his ministers do the same. What makes this so affective is that with the natural eye or carnal mind you can't see the difference. With the spiritual eye you will be able to recognize Satan and his ministers.

Jesus said my sheep hear my voice and a stranger they will not follow. How then does this transformation into light affect God's children and the children of the world? His ultimate plan is to keep the children of the world from converting into children of God, and to keep the children of God from maturing spiritually.

Have you ever heard the saying if it walks like a duck and quacks like a duck then it must be a duck? You have to be very careful about that type of thinking. The outward presentation of people can fool you. There are professional church goers that will fool you into believing they are saved.

They are faithful every Sunday. They sing in the choir. They are on the deacon board, the usher board, and even in the pulpit. They preform every week. You automatically think they are saved.

It's dangerous to judge a book by its cover because you don't always get what you see. Have you noticed that there are churches in just about every neighborhood? Some even have three or four on one block. With all the churches that are open, and all the preaching going on, you would think that the whole world should be saved.

Satan in his transforming stage, he opens up churches, and raises his own apostles, preachers, prophets, and other leaders to deceive you. They will give you a watered-down version of the bible. They will fill your ears with the things you want to hear and give you none of the things you need for spiritual growth. There only concern is to convince you that the purpose of going to church is to have a good time.

They will not preach against sin. Certain sins

they will stay away from because they need you to keep coming back. All you will get from them are messages of prosperity and blessings. They will tell you only good things are coming, and your breakthrough is on the way. Understand we live in the flesh, and that type of preaching goes right along with what the flesh wants to hear. It's what makes it so easy for Satan and his ministers to keep people off track.

This flesh does not like to suffer. It hates difficulty, pain, and any kind of heartache. All the flesh wants is a good feeling all the time, and there is not any growth apart from suffering. Satan knows this as well. He keeps feeding you with messages of blessings and prosperity. The messages that Satan and his ministers bring will never have the power of conviction in them. Satan doesn't want you to examine yourself. He only wants you thinking that you don't deserve what's going on with you. Your breakthrough is on the way.

Most children of God don't look at suffering as an opportunity to grow and develop spiritual attributes. They look at suffering as a hindrance. They fool themselves into believing that they can do more for God if it wasn't there. What the Lord allows because of his grace is sufficient in time of need.

In addition to a watered-down gospel, Satan will also mimic God in gift giving. You actually believe it came from God, but Satan gave it to you. James 1:17 reads "every good gift and every perfect gift is from above and come down from the father lights, with whom is no variableness, neither shadow of turning." How then do children of God misconstrue the gifts they receive from Satan? For some reason we simply refuse to believe that we would ever except anything coming from Satan. We don't fully understand what a good gift from God is.

Most people are under the impression that a good gift is something that they like. If they like it then it had to come from God. We fail to realize that God will give us a good gift that we don't like. We don't like it, so we reject it and think it came from Satan. We are backwards in our thinking. Satan will never give you anything you don't like. God will never give you anything that goes against his word whether you like it or not.

Let me share this personal testimony with you. When I started working for Wal-Mart ten years ago, I had in mind that I wanted to be a manager. I had management experience in restaurants, so they were going to fast track me. A position came available for Zone Manager and part of the requirements was to work every third Sunday and Wednesday. That would mean that I would end up missing Sunday service and Bible Class once a month. At the time I was an associate minister.

I went and talked to my Pastor and told him about the position and what it required. He told me it would be ok if I took the job because I'm not pastoring. I took the job and things went well for a little while. Then all hell broke loose in my life. I didn't know if I was coming or going. My dreams, my goals, my desires to promote myself caused me to make a foolish decision. I was fully aware of the fact that God would not give me anything that would keep me from my service to him. My mind was blinded, and I began to justify my decision. The more I justified it the worse things became. Needless to say, I ended up getting terminated and back to square one.

Have you ever wondered how Satan knows us so well? He doesn't know your thoughts nor can he read your mind. Think about this for a minute. Ever since you learned how to talk, what have you been talking about? All we talk about is what we like or don't like, what we want or don't want. That has been and still is the basis of our conversation. It's easy to learn a person who was as self-consumed as I was. He knew my goals, my desires, and dreams. It wasn't hard for him to set a trap and I fell in headfirst.

The closer I got to obtaining my personal goals the further I got away from God. That made the whole experience vanity. Before I close this chapter let me share this with you. God will never give you anything that will take you away from what you are doing for him. I know that we dream big. I know that we have goals that we want to reach. Just make sure that your dreams and goals draw you closer to God and not drive you further away.

Chapter 3 He Teams Up with Self

Have you ever said or heard of the phrase, "the devil made me do it?" Satan may have teamed up with your carnal mind and put the thought there, but he can't make you do anything. We are created to be free moral agents which means we decide what we will or will not do. Even when persuaded the decision is ours. I know it's easier to put the blame on others, but if you ever want to get to where God wants you to be, you have to start looking at self. Self is Satan's doorway.

As long as Satan can keep you thinking it's the other person, you will keep ignoring your role in the situation. You may even incorporate in your prayer life for God to change the other person. The self-pride that we have will always see the fault in others long before seeing it in ourselves. Satan has the power to blind your mind so that you can't see yourself. The only person that will cause you to see yourself is our Lord Jesus Christ. That's why you hear so many people say you don't have to go to church to be saved. Satan doesn't want you to be exposed to the word of God, because he knows that the word has power to change hearts. Changed heart leads to a changed life.

The carnal mind is in darkness and he doesn't want any light coming to your mind. You feel that you don't have to go to church. He directs you to one of his churches and that's how he keeps you in darkness. Light will cause you to see him for who he is. He doesn't want you to see him. If Satan can keep you from seeing he can keep you from growing up in the Lord.

Have you ever seen a church member that has been in church over twenty tears and will get upset if you sit in their seat? You may know a deacon who gets upset because somebody else is singing his song, or a preacher who gets upset because another preacher is preaching a sermon that he has preached. Even while you are sitting in church Satan is busy blocking your mind from hearing the word of God. Satan knows we have short attention spans, so he puts thoughts in your mind while the word is being preached.

The preacher is preaching his heart out and we are sitting there thinking about everything but Jesus. Satan's ultimate goal is to stop the spread of the gospel. If he can keep you from hearing it that's one less person, he has to worry about. I have been told by church going people "I hope you heard what the preacher said" as though the word was just for me and didn't apply to them.

Self all by itself is a mess. Paul says in the seventh chapter of Romans "o wretched man that I am", because he recognized that no clean thing dwells in this flesh. You are what the young people call a hot mess. If all you can see is the fault in others; it is a sure indication that your mind is blinded by Satan and the only one who can give you insight is Jesus. You have to want to see yourself.

As long as you measure yourself by your own standards you will always look good to yourself. You have to measure yourself by the word of God. What does God say about you? Then you will begin to see how ugly you really are. Adding light will cause you to see deeper into you, and that's the reality many people don't want to know about themselves. I don't want to see the ugly in me, so I stay away from the one thing that will cause me to see it.

Don't be afraid of examining yourself, because of what you are going to see. You can't grow in the Lord apart from seeing who you truly are. Not only in teaming up with the flesh will he block your mind, but there are other tactics he uses against us to keep us from moving forward and growing in the Lord.

Think back to when you first received your calling from God, and you shared it with people. How did they respond to the news? You have some that were excited, and you have some that were negative, and generally it's the ones closest to you that are negative. You walked away from them questioning the very calling God placed on your life. Satan has just caused you to feel discouraged. You got up the courage to preach, teach, or sing for the first time and it didn't go the way you thought it should have gone, and you walked away feeling discouraged.

Discourage – to deprive of courage, hope, or confidence; to advise or persuade a person to refrain; to prevent or try to prevent by disapproving or raising objections or obstacles. In your walk with the Lord which one of these definitions did Satan use on you. There is something on the inside of us that wants to be accepted. When we do what we do we want people to be pleased with it. If they are not pleased with it, we are liable to give up and quit. Satan knows if he can get you to think you can't do it then you will not do it. If he can't get in your mind to discourage you then he will use others to discourage you.

As God's child you need to remember that God is the only one you have to please. The bible nowhere tells us we have to be pleasing to man. God told Jeremiah not to be afraid of the looks on their faces. This means they are not going to like what you are saying to them. Anytime you make a stand and say what God tells you to say you are going to anger people. People will try to discourage you. Recognize you don't wrestle with flesh and blood.

Learn to see that Satan is somewhere behind the scenes messing with the hearts and minds of people trying to stop them from the work of the Lord. Even in writing this book I've encountered negative people, obstacles, and time distractions to keep me from writing. I just pray to God that he keeps me in perfect peace. God promises that he will give you peace that surpasses all understanding that will guard my heart and mind. I can handle all that Satan shoots at me because God has me in his hands. I don't get bent out of shape when things don't go the way I think they should. I have learned that God is working behind the scenes in my favor.

Think for a minute, when things start working against you be mindful not to allow discouragement to set in. It could lead to frustration which is another method Satan will use against you. Frustrate- to cause to have no effect, bring to nothing, counteract, nullify; to prevent from achieving an objective, foil, baffle; to prevent gratifying certain impulses or desires, either conscious or unconscious.

I wonder if I counted all the times, I threw my hands up in the air and said, "I give up!" what would that number be? All the things that can get in the way of what you are trying to achieve can drive you to a point of throwing in the towel. We want every situation in life to be good and make us feel good. When a monkey wrench is thrown into our program it knocks us off of our square. Whether it's a job, marriage, friendship, church, or even a vacation, we want everything to be smooth sailing.

I remember early in my ministry I wanted to quit. My marriage was on the rocks. I couldn't keep a job for a long period of time, and my family was all in my business. It seemed everywhere I turned there was trouble. I had my mind made up that I was going to quit preaching because I couldn't handle all the pressure. I had gotten so frustrated I couldn't see straight.

I remember going to church with my hand on my wallet. I was going to give my license back to Pastor Williams. When I stepped in his office to open my mouth, he told me I was preaching that morning. I said, "yes sir." turned around and left his office. Inside I was a complete mess. I asked God at that moment what in the world are you doing to me. God told me to trust in him. He said, "this is a battle that you can't fight by yourself, so stop trying and place it in my hands."

A great calm came over my spirit. I allowed the hurt, pain, and stress to frustrate me to the point of giving up on the very one my help was coming from. I know we want things to be good all the time, but we have to recognize that things are going to happen to frustrate you. Remember that on the other side of the frustration stands a blessing for you if you hang in there. Satan uses frustration for the purpose of destruction, but God uses frustration for the purpose of growing you up in the faith.

As children of God, it is vital that we view frustration as an opportunity to grow and not one to give up. If you are not careful the frustration will lead to confusion. Confuse- to mix up, jumble together, put in disorder; to mix up mentally, bewilder, perplex, to fail to distinguish between.

Pastor Williams asked this question in one of

the classes he was teaching "have you ever heard anyone say they want a divorce because their spouse is too good to them?" I have found in life that as long as things are going well and we are happy getting what we want, we will hang right there with it. When the table turns, and all hell breaks loose we are now looking for a way out.

Have you ever been to the point that you wanted to leave and stay at the same time? You are so confused because when it's good, it's good, and when it's bad, it's bad. You couldn't make up your mind because you were stuck between doing the right thing and relieving the stress. The right thing to do is stay and work it out, but it is so much easier to just walk away from it. You have two kinds of counsel going on in your life. One is saying, "If I were you, I wouldn't stay?" The other is saying, "Stay and work it out." What do you do? Whose voice screams the loudest inside of you. Who do you listen to? Sounds to me like frustration is causing you confusion.

As I previously mentioned I was ready to turn in my license. I allowed frustration to cause confusion in my life. I had made up my mind that I was giving up preaching and going to live a normal life. Whatever that meant. My mind was cloudy, and I couldn't see my way through. When Pastor Williams told me that I was preaching, I was able to see God for who he is. I was ready to give up on God, but God didn't give up on me. (another shouting moment) Now as I look back on that situation, I see how it was necessary for me to go through it at that time.

The intrinsic value of suffering outweighs all the silver and gold the world has to offer. It didn't feel good while I was going through, but it all worked out for my good. You have to learn to trust that God is able. It's all in his plan for your life. Learn to see what discouragement, frustration, and confusion is designed to do in your life. Remember Satan wants to use them to destroy you, but God wants to use them to build you up and strengthen you in him.

As I close out this chapter remember that when Satan tries to team up with your flesh just keep in mind what the scripture teaches. Greater is he that is with in me than he that is in the world.

Chapter 4 He Teams Up with The World System

There is a question that has been raised, "are all secular things sinful?" Secular- relating to worldly things as distinguished from things relating to church and religion. Are God's children allowed to use secular things for their personal benefit? How does Satan team up with secular things? 1 Corinthians 6:12 and 10:23 Paul states that all things are lawful to him, but all things are not expedient, but all things edify not, but I will not be brought under the power of any, and also in Rom. 14:16 let not then your good be evil spoken of.

There are obvious ways that we recognize

Satan moving in the world system. He uses our own weakness against us. He knows what we like, and he knows how to present it. You are aware of the basic do's and don'ts in life because they are covered in God's commandments. Paul lists them the in Galatians 5. You know to stay away from those things.

Married people know to drink water from their own well, single people know not to have sex before marriage, and children know to be obedient to their parents. Knowing and doing are two different things. You can see Satan behind it all. I want to look at how he uses legitimate things against us. Things that may not be sin can become sin if not handled properly.

If we all did as Jesus commanded and love one another this problem would be eliminated. Since we don't, it becomes a problem. Have you ever made this statement? "I am grown." Maybe you've made this one, "I don't care what people think about me." I have and it has gotten me in trouble with God.

Life is not always black or white. There is a grey area in life where the struggle is. You can't pinpoint it as a yes or no because it could be a maybe. Remember when I stated earlier in the book, if Satan can't get you to do the wrong thing, he will get you to do the right thing in the wrong way? This statement fits in the grey area of life.

People have been arguing for a long time about grey area issues. Just to name a few of them: drinking, dancing, shooting pool, playing cards, and hobbies as fishing, bowling, and other sport activities. I am not going to talk about all of them, but the same principle can be applied to each of them.

I believe every child of God loves doing things in the grey area of life. They are secular things, and it doesn't mean they are wrong. The problem comes into play with how you use them. God asked Cain, "where is your brother Abel?" Cain responded by asking, "am I my brother's keeper?"

That's the attitude Satan will attack when you are operating in the grey areas of life. You don't care what people think, and you don't care how they feel because you are grown, and you can do what you want.

Romans 14:21 reads "it is good neither to eat flesh, nor to drink wine, nor anything whereby thy brother stumbleth or is offended, or is made weak." As a child of God, you cannot afford to have that I'm grown mentality. Satan will team up with that and cause what you are doing to become sin. You are exploiting your brother's weakness.

At Greater Morning Star MBC Pastor Williams allowed me to teach new members class. One of the examples I would use was this. It's Saturday morning and I have a taste for some orange juice. I go to Kroger in the Devington shopping plaza to get some. When I get in the store, I noticed the lines are long and they are short on cashiers. I am in a rush. I don't have time to wait. and I noticed the liquor store in front of the plaza. I go over there. I go into the liquor store and buy my orange juice and go about my business. You may ask if there was anything wrong with what I did? Let me continue the story.

Consider you are the new member. You are walking down the sidewalk and see your new members class teacher coming out of the liquor store with a brown bag in his hand. What thoughts are going to run through your mind. Will you come back and listen to me teach you?

Just because we have freedom to do what we want to; we must be careful to not let our freedoms cause someone else to fall. My decision should have been either wait in line or leave out the orange juice all together. You are your brother's keeper. It does matter what people think about you. You have to be careful about how you use the grey areas in life. Don't let your good be evil spoken of.

I hear people say all the time I don't drink, smoke, party, or do drugs anymore. That is a great thing, but it doesn't stop with the do's and don'ts. There are so many ways Satan comes at us.

There is one more point about the grey area we need to look at. It deals with how we handle things in the grey area. When I was a little boy my daddy would take me fishing. I didn't know what time we were going, but I knew what day we would go. My dad worked Monday through Friday, and we went to church on Sundays. That left Saturday for fishing.

My dad taught me at an early age that you don't put anything before your service to God. He was so adamant about this that he would turn down triple pay at work, so he could go to church on Sunday. Anybody that knows me knows that I love to fish, but I will not go fishing when it comes to my service to God. No matter what you have going on in your life, or in the lives of your children, nothing is to come before your service to God.

Solomon said what does it profit a man to gain the whole world and die and lose your soul.

Secular success grants no spiritual rewards. When you die, they die with you. Why sacrifice service to God for something that is vanity. I know we love our children, careers, and activities, but they have their proper place. And that is to not be put before God. Satan will team up with your activities and cause you to justify within yourself that it's ok to miss one Sunday.

The first Sunday you miss will trouble you, but it makes it easier to miss another. Before you know it, you've been out for six months without even giving it a second thought. Be careful because the grey areas in life can become sin for you if you cause your brother to stumble or be offended. If you put them before you put your service to God.

Grow past the obvious methods of attack and start seeing the subtle ways Satan moves against you. Remember his ultimate goal is to stop the spread of the gospel of Jesus Christ, and he will use anything or anybody he can to accomplish his goal. Enjoy the grey areas in life but be careful

He's Not Your Friend

how you use them. You don't want your good evil spoken of.

Chapter 5 He's Seeking to Kill You

1 Peter 5:8 reads *"be sober, be vigilant; because your adversary the devil, as a roaring lion, walketh about seeking whom he may devour"*. As God's children we need to always keep it at our attention that Satan wants to kill us. He wants us dead, and the only reason we are still alive is because God won't let him kill us. (another shouting moment)

Remember what his ultimate goal is. God won't let kill you physically, but Satan will try to kill your reputation and destroy the power of your testimony. As leaders of God's people, we are under constant attack whether we be male or female. Peter says to be sober and vigilant because that will keep you focused. You will be able to see the lion when he is on the prowl. As leaders we have a responsibility to not only feed the sheep, but also protect them from the lion. In order to protect the sheep, you must make sure that you are in good standing with God, focused, and prepared for battle.

Satan is a shrewd task master, and he knows when and how to attack. He knows how long it's been since you read or studied your bible. He knows how long it's been since you last prayed. He is fully aware of your weakness and knows when you are at your weakest point in life. Satan knows not to strike when you are strong. He waits till life has kicked you around a bit and then he strikes. It's in those moments of weakness that temptation becomes a challenge, and you have to be careful not to give in because one slip, one fall. One moment of yielding to temptation can destroy your whole ministry and cause many people to fall along with you.

As leaders we need to understand that our reputations arrive at the place long before we get there. Think back to when the announcement clerk announced revival week. What happened when they announced the speakers who are coming? Automatically people started thinking about what kind of preacher are they. They have made up their mind on who they are coming to hear and who they aren't. Some are bold enough to ask the Pastor why he chose certain preachers.

Your reputation speaks volumes about who you are. Satan knows that the better your reputation is the more influence you will have, and the more power you add to your testimony. He really wants you dead, but since he can't kill you, he tries to find ways of destroying your testimony. Every straight man knows that our greatest weakness on the planet is women.

As a straight man I could say, if God made anything better than a woman, he kept it for himself. I am sure every straight man would agree with me on that. Ever since the creation of woman men have been falling because of their love for women, and it's still going on today. Leaders be very careful when it comes to handling women. You must guard how you speak to them, how you look at them, and how you cause them to feel about you.

They are not your property, nor are they a piece of meat that you can use for your pleasure and throw away. They are to be respected, loved, and cared for. They were given to us to walk along the side of us to help us where we fall short. Even with all that being said we still have a weakness and Satan knows how to set a trap for us.

He knows what is going on in our home. He knows what's going on in your bedroom. He knows what's going on at church. He knows what's going on at work. He knows when you are at your weakest point. He knows who to send your way. When teaching a class for men I often use this illustration.

My cousin Tony and I was setting up one at his father's houses and we noticed a field mouse had gotten in the house. I got a mouse trap and told Tony to get some peanut butter. I put the peanut butter on the trap; set the trap in the floor and turned off the kitchen lights. I told Tony to be quit and watch what happens.

We sat quietly and sure enough the mouse came out. It ran up to the trap and smelled the peanut butter and ran off. Tony said it didn't work. I told him to be patient. Sure, enough the mouse came back out and ran up to the trap and smelled the peanut butter and ran off again. It must have done it three or four times. The last time it came out and went to smell the peanut butter as it did the other times, but this time it jumped on the trap and got caught.

That is how subtle of a trap Satan sets for us. Things are not going well at home. You are arguing and fussing with your wife. She sleeps in the bed and you are on the couch. The intimacy you once shared is not happening and you are frustrated. You don't have any thoughts of leaving because you love your wife. But you are not happy with the way things are going. One evening after fussing you decide that you want some ice cream. You looked in the freezer and there wasn't any. So, you go to the store to get some. While in the store getting the ice cream you hear your name called and you look up and it's an old friend from high school. She comes and speaks to you.

You and your high school friend have a basic conversation that doesn't last a minute. She says as you are leaving it was good to see you. You leave and go home not even giving the encounter a second thought. Situations at home are still the same. You have run out of ice cream again and you go back to the store to get some. Guess who you see again in the store. That old friend you bumped into the last time.

This time the conversation gets a little more personal. You tell her that you are married with children and she tells you that she is single. You get your ice cream and go home. Situations at home are still the same and you have run out of ice cream again. You go to the store to get some more and guess who you bump into again. This time the conversation gets even more personal. You start telling her how things are between you and your wife and she lends you her ear. She gives you her number and lets you know that anytime you want to talk just give her a call.

You get your ice cream and go home. Situations at home are still the same and you are out of ice cream again and this time when you go to the store, you're looking for her. Sure, enough you see her, and she says to you, "I was expecting your call." You say to her, "I couldn't call from home, but I would like to talk."

"I just live around corner you can come over and talk if you want to."

So, you go over and end up doing more than talking. You have now jumped on the trap. It may not kill you physically, but you have just destroyed your marriage. If you are a Pastor you destroy your ministry, you hurt your children and everyone else that loved and followed you. Leaders simply cannot walk around with blinders on. You have to be able to see every trap that Satan is setting.

How do you do that? Psalms 119:105 reads *"thy word is a lamp unto my feet and a light unto my path".* You must read, you must study, you must stay close to God if you are going to see the subtle traps set before you. There is nothing worse and I mean nothing worse than a LAZY PREACHER WHO WILL NOT READ OR STUDY GODS WORD.

Keep in mind if you lose your testimony with people you may never get it back. Leaders Satan is coming for you, and you have to be on guard at all time. You also have to know how to fight him off. You can't do that if you don't know who you are fighting. We will be spending time in the next chapter understanding who we are fighting.

Chapter 6 Understand Who You Are Fighting

Ephesians. 6: reads *"for we wrestle not against flesh and blood, but against principalities, against powers, against the rulers of the darkness of this world, against spiritual wickedness in high places"*. I heard it said that the greatest trick that the devil has pulled off is getting people to believe that he doesn't exist. I say there is another trick that is better than that. He fools God's children into believing that their battle is with flesh and blood.

It's sad to say that God's children will fuss and fight in the church. We underestimate the power that Satan has. We can't see him for who he is. We have no idea of how to defend ourselves against him. We plot and plan on how we are going to get even with one another. Satan is sitting back laughing at us because he knows that he is whipping you. You are blaming someone else. I don't mind taking a whipping for something I did. I don't want to take a whipping for someone else.

I remember some years ago when I was playing basketball with a group of friends. I kept getting into it with David not knowing that David was already upset about something at home. We were bumping and pushing each other under the basket. David stopped, looked at me, and said "This whipping is not meant for you." I stepped back and said, "I feel you and left him alone."

As God's children you would think we would have sense enough to recognize who we are fighting. God tells us in his word who we are fighting. Yet and still, we won't listen. Why can't we see Satan moving? Why are we so busy looking at other people? How can the children of light be blinded by darkness? The answer is we live in the physical realm. We tend to think that the physical things in life are the problem. If God's children could only see that the warfare is not physical, but spiritual then families wouldn't fight like they do. The divorce rate wouldn't be so high. Fights in the church wouldn't be taking place.

This challenge is real. It's hard to look past the physical confrontations that we are faced with and see that it's not a physical issue. If we could see Satan with our physical eye, then we would know how and when to fight him. We have been trained to fight what we see. We have been taught ungodly principles by those that reared us up.

What did your parents tell you to do if someone hit you? If they were like mine, they told you to hit them back. We are trained to fight the physical fight at an early age. Jesus said if someone hit you on the cheek, turn the other cheek. We will take the advice of our parents because after all that's what we want to do anyway. We have been trained all of our lives to fight the physical. Now that we are saved, we are told not to fight the physical because the physical is not the problem.

The problem with that is we can't see the spiritual. We don't know how to fight the spiritual, because we haven't been trained on how to fight the spiritual fight. How can you learn to fight the spiritual fight when you see the Pastor is fighting the deacons, choir members fighting over songs, ushers fighting over what post to stand, and pew members fight over seats?

You are faced with physical fights everywhere you go in life. Why are you now expected to fight spiritually? God tells you that your fight is not with flesh and blood. God is letting you know there is a powerful force that you can't see with your physical eye. You have to learn how to fight and it's going to go against everything you know how to do. All we have been taught is physical. Now we have to put all that aside and learn the spiritual.

Put what momma and daddy told you aside and do what Jesus said. Turn the other cheek and in doing so you are fighting the spiritual fight. It's not about getting the physical victories. They are going to pass away. The spiritual victories will follow you into glory and will never pass away. Once you have been trained to fight the spiritual fight things are going to change for the better. Your relationships with people will get better. Your attitude gets better. The way you treat people will get better. The way you talk will get better. The stress and worry will leave.

This is what I am trying to get you to see. When you fight the physical fight, your life stays in turmoil. There isn't any spiritual growth taking place. When you fight the spiritual fight, you grow spiritually. Tour physical life calms down. Satan doesn't want you to see him for who he is, so he can continue to wreak havoc on your life. That's when your bad days outweigh your good days.

When you see him for who he is your good days will outweigh your bad days. Your fight is not against me, and my fight is not against you. There is another force behind the scenes moving in ways that it is impossible to see with your physical eye. Your mind may be blinded, and you can't see him, but you don't have to stay that way. Pray and ask God to open your eyes to see Satan for who he is. Ask God for discernment to see when Satan is using others. When he is using you. The next time someone does something to offend you, you will be able to see Satan and not the other person. It will make a huge difference in how you handle the situation.

Remember fighting the physical fight will cost you more in the long run, but when you let God fight for you, you will gain more in the long run. As I close out this chapter, I want to leave you with this thought. I know it's hard to stand there quietly while people are giving you a piece of their mind. I pray this scripture will do for you what it did for me. You will find it in Job chapter 6:24 and it reads *"Teach me, and I will hold my tongue; and cause me to understand wherein I have erred"*.

He's Not Your Friend

Chapter 7 He's Not to Be Feared

2 Tim. 1:7 reads *"For God hath not given us the spirit of fear, but of power, and love, and of a sound mind."* 1 John 4:4 reads *"Ye are of God little and have overcome them; because greater is he that is within you than he that is in the world.* After everything that has been pinned about Satan, I don't want anyone to worry about what he can or can't do. There is no need to fear him. Yes, he is a great power, and yes, he is more powerful than we are, but we don't have to be afraid of him.

When you look at the two scriptures that this chapter starts with it gives you all the encouragement you need to fully understand that you can make it. I have been fighting the desire to preach in this book, but when I think about the fact that God has me in his hands it makes me want to shout. Do you think that Satan is pleased with me writing this book? Do you think that he wants to be exposed? Do you think he wants you to gain an understanding of who he is? I am sure that he is trying to kill me right now, but I don't give it a second thought.

The God I serve is greater than any force around and nothing can or will happen to me unless God allows it. So, since God laid it in my heart to write this book and God gave me the insight into Satan to write this book. God has the power to control the outcome of this book being written. I have no need to fear or worry about Satan. One of the many things I've learned in my walk with God is that I have absolutely have nothing to fear.

Even though there are things that happen to frighten me for a moment, my mind reflects on the fact that I am in God's hands. That brings a great calm over me. I recognize that fear doesn't come from God. It's another one of the methods Satan will use against you. Satan knows that if you are afraid chances are you will not do it. If you allow it, fear will stop you. Fear will stop you from doing what God called you to do.

I received my calling to preach in September of 1993. I went to Pastor Williams and asked him, "How do you know you are called to preach?" He said to me, "If you still feel the same way in thirty days come back and talk to me." I didn't go back. I didn't want to preach. I didn't like getting up in front of people to talk. I allowed Satan to fill my heart and mind with doubt and fear. I ran from God. I thought that could get me out of preaching.

After all the suffering I went through, I went back to Pastor Williams in December of 1995 and asked him the same question. "How do you know when God is calling you to preach?" He gave me the same answer as before. If you feel the same way in thirty days come and talk to me again. This time I went back, and I gave my trial sermon June 14, 1996.

I've had my battles with Satan over the years, but with the help of the Lord he has delivered me from all of them. I know that in life we all find ourselves faced with fear. It may be a bad report from the doctor, the loss of a loved one, the loss of a job, or having your first child, or going on your first date, the first day of kindergarten, or even being baptized. Fear shows up in all kinds of situations in life.

You can't stop fear from coming in, but you can keep fear from stopping you. keep in mind there isn't any courage apart from fear. The bible encourages us throughout scripture to be of a good courage, because God knows that we will have to face our fears. When you have confidence in God even though fear may be present you know God has you no matter what happens. That gives you the courage to press forward.

Satan uses fear to stop you, but God uses fear

to develop your trust and confidence in him. Romans 8:31 Reads "What *shall we say to these things? If God be for us, who can be against us*"? With God on my side, I don't have to worry about anything or anyone. God has me hedged in, and he has Cherubim's guarding me and no power on earth can get to me unless God say so. (shouting and praising)

I can walk with my head held high because God is with me. I can speak with boldness because God is with me. I can treat my neighbor right because God is with me. I can love my enemies because God is with me. I can praise him in the morning, noon, or night because no weapon that is formed against me shall prosper. I'm more than a conqueror because God is with me.

There is no need to worry about what Satan is trying to do to you. That battle is not yours. Trust that God has you in his hands and know that you can make it. My prayer is that this book will be a blessing to your life. I pray it encourages your heart and mind to trust in the Lord Jesus Christ. I would be remiss if I closed this book without extending an invitation to come to Jesus.

The scripture says for God so loves the world that he gave his only begotten son, that whosoever believe in him should not perish, but have everlasting life. Jesus willing gave his life so that you can have life. He was nailed to the cross, and he died on the cross. They put him in a borrowed tomb, and it was very early Sunday morning he got up out of the grave. He is alive and well.

Salvation can be yours just for the asking. If you confess with your mouth and believe in your heart that God raised him from the dead, thou shalt be saved. Come to Jesus while you have time. May God forever bless and keep you is my prayer.

www.ingramcontent.com/pod-product-compliance
Lightning Source LLC
Chambersburg PA
CBHW052122110526
44592CB00013B/1712